I0480422

1

FOREWORD

Product Management is defined very differently in every organization. It can cover Product Development, New Product Development, Product Marketing or Product Management.

This book intends to define the product manager's role in the conception of a product through to the end of life for that product. Significant effort is spent by the Product Manager in creating a product strategy and a product roadmap and the first step to tactically execute on that product strategy. While this book touches on both these topics, they are covered in detail in Product Roadmap and Product Strategy books available on Amazon. This book will walk you through step-by-step process required to successfully take a product idea to the market and eventually turndown the product to make room for the next generation of product.

PREFACE

In todays fast pace development, agile development, continuous integration etc. a product leader needs the ability to take a product idea rapidly from a concept phase to launch in the market. The Product Manager needs to continue assessing the product, to ensure it is meeting its success criteria, generating a profit and eventually turning down the product. This book walks you through every step in the process as well as discusses typical challenges and blind spots that a product manager might overlook.

The book focuses on a real world approach to delivering the product, i.e., provides tools that you can leverage in your day to day product management role in any organization. This is based on over 23 years of product management experience spread across North America and Asia in both start-up and large scale organizational environments.

WHO IS THIS BOOK FOR?

This book is aimed at software product managers, product owners, product marketing prime, product analyst, project managers, marketing managers, scrum masters, and leaders of product teams (Director or VP of Product Management). If you are in a leadership position and want the team to build a software product you need an instrument to align the different parts of the organization. This instrument is Product Management.

This book is aimed at readers with all levels of product experience. If you are working on your very first product idea you can follow each step, use tools indicated and take your idea through the execution and launch phase. If you are a veteran you can take away solutions to the different challenges raised, learn about how to build alignment and support for your product concept.

If you are a product director or responsible for a portfolio of products, likely you already have a well-developed "definition and process for Product Management", you can use this book to ensure your process covers every aspect of product management and fill any gaps in the process. This book starts with a review of Product Life Cycle, Product Adoption and Project life cycle and further delves into the role of a Product Manager at each stage of the product.

HOW TO USE THIS BOOK

This book is based on my experience and the sequence of elements noted is what worked best within the different organizations I worked with. Having said that, there is no right sequence depending on your organization structure, culture etc., you may prioritize some elements over others.

The elements that we will cover in this book are:

What is a Product Life Cycle?
What is Project Life Cycle? How does these work together?
How do you build a roadmap for a new idea?
How do you validate your product idea?
How do you build a business case for your product idea?
How do you prioritize the features for your product development?
What can you do at project kick off, to ensure success of the project?
How do you govern the project to ensure success?
What are the responsibilities of a product manager vs project manager?
How does a product manager ensure a successful product launch?
How does a product manager support product marketing?
What are the post launch KPIs to ensure product success?
What are the turndown options at the end of the product life cycle?
What are the typical blind spots a product manager should be

aware and prevent?

CHAPTER 1: PRODUCT MANAGEMENT OVERVIEW

A Product Manager's role is to support a product at every stage of its product life cycle. It is a leadership role that brings the supporting teams required to profitably support the product in the market.

A product manager needs to ensure that the product gets all the required support from the organization. In a start-up environment, a product manager likely will have more autonomy and be able to wear multiple hats (product manager, marketing, pricing, trainer etc.) vs. in a larger organization the product manager may work with primes from the marketing, pricing, training teams.

A product manager should be seen as the "conductor directing a musical performance", where each part of the organization is a part of the orchestra. In an organization where the product manager is complaining "I have no time to work on strategy", the likely scenario is the product manager is busy filling holes in the orchestra rather than conducting the orchestra. Key part of the leadership role of a product manager is to highlight the gaps and fill the gaps for their product.

Depending on the Product Life-Cycle stage, Product Adoption stage and Project Life Cycle the actual work a product manager would do is different. Typically there is a strong correlation between Product Life-Cycle and Product Adoption stage, while the Project Life Cycle is typically before the product is built or when moving from one gate to another. In this section let's look at Product Life-Cycle and Product Adoption stages and overlay Project Life Cycle on those, the later chapters would walk through a Product Manager role at each stage. If you are familiar with these theoretical concepts you can jump ahead to chapter two "Ideation".

Product Life-Cycle Management

Product life-cycle management is the set of strategies a product manager applies as the product moves through its lifecycle.

A typical product life-cycle is

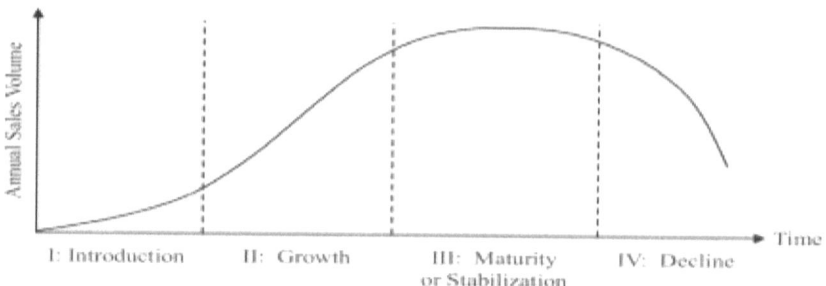

Source: https://en.m.wikipedia.org/wiki/Product_life-cycle_management_(marketing)

The different stages are characterized by the following behavior:

Characteristics	Stages			
	Introduction	**Growth**	**Maturity**	**Decline**
Sales	Low	High	High	Low
Investment	Very High	High	Low	Low
Competition	Low to None	High	Very High	Very High
Profit	Low	High	High	Low
Product Version	MVP	Multiple Version	Full Product Line	Survival of Fittest
Product Marketing	Educational	Competitive Difference	Why Us	Minimal Marketing
Product Pricing	Market Penetration pricing	Priced to Gain Share	Defend Position pricing	Ensure Profitability

Introduction is the stage of really testing the product idea, releasing the minimum viable product to get an understanding of what features resonate, and testing the pricing in the market. A true introductory product does not have a direct competition (or the competition is "do nothing").

Growth is the stage where the product has resonated in the market, Product Manager develops a feature rich product. As the product resonates in the market, your competitors will build a similar product or new competition enters the market, higher competition results in pricing needing to be set to gain market share (unless otherwise dictated by your product/organization strategy).

Maturity is the stage where the product manager is not adding many new features, but rather the profits from the product are being used to fund other products. The product has little investment, and hence the profitability is the highest at this stage of the product. Most customers are aware of the product capabilities and the marketing is focused not on educating the customers on the feature set, rather it is on "Why" purchase from your organization.

Decline is the stage where you have the product but few customers are still buying the product. The Product Manager is just keeping the product alive, minimal investment is made into the product. The Product Manager is spending time on planning the exit strategies, communication plan around the exit strategy and how to migrate the customer to another product (or sell substitute etc. based on the strategy).

Product Adoption

The technology adoption lifecycle is a sociological model that describes the adoption of a new product, according to the demographic and psychological characteristics of defined adopter groups.

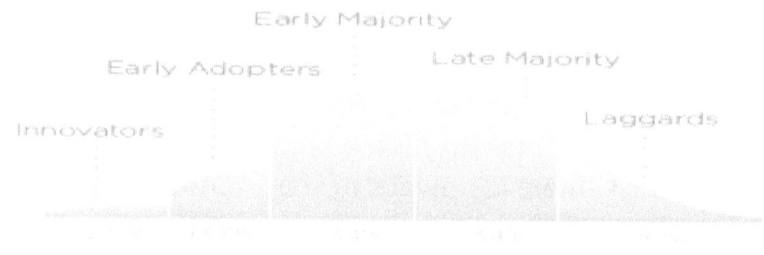

INNOVATION ADOPTION LIFECYCLE

The above Rogers Bell Curve comes from Everett M Rogers, Diffusion of Innovation theory.

While the original version of the Rogers Bell curve was aimed at farms in late 1950's, the modern interpretation is as follows:

Innovators: The cohort of customers willing to try new ideas (will usually go and find a solution, it is like a hobby), willing to risk trying new elements, providing feedback and comfortable with having a more complex setup basis. Willing to hack solutions together and usually not price sensitive.

Early Adopters: This cohort of customers hear about new ideas and are quick to understand the benefits of the technology and try the product. They are also comfortable with a complex setup process (or incomplete product) as long as it works.

Early Majority: This cohort of customers are expecting a complete product, assured that it works, easy to set up and good support.

Late Majority: This cohort of customers only come onboard when it is a well-established product, no question about its success, lots of folks are using it etc. This is no risk associated with the product.

Laggards: This is the cohort of customers who are using this product only because other substitutes do not exist, or they are forced to use it because everybody else is using it.

As a product addresses each cohort of the customer above it achieves 100% of market penetration (see graph below). Product Managers needs to be aware of which cohort of customer is being targeted by the product as that reflects the expectation of the customer for the product, marketing message, pricing etc., over the lifecycle of the product.

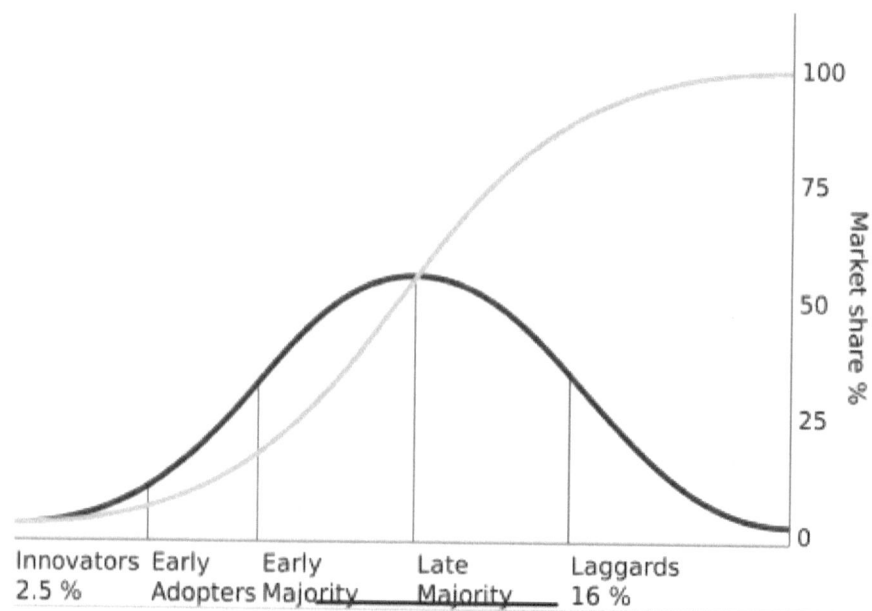

Crossing The Chasm

A variation of the Product Adoption cycle was proposed by Geoffrey Moore in Crossing the Chasm: Marketing and Selling High-Tech Products to Mainstream Customers.

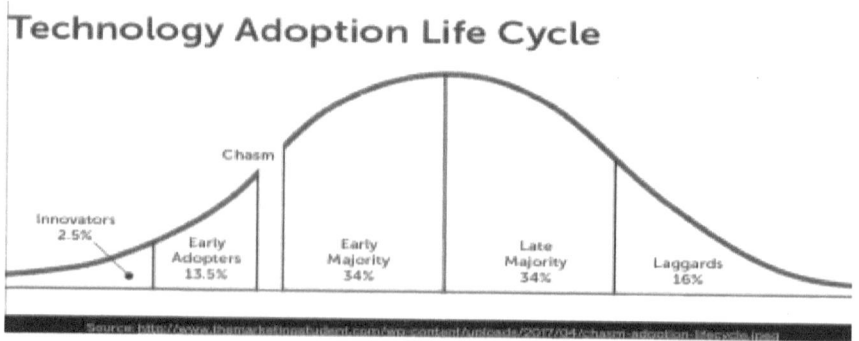

While there are gaps between each segment, the largest gap is between Early Adopters and Early Majority. The Early Majority, also called "Pragmatist" in the book, have very different expectations from Early Adopters. They are expecting a product (not just a technical/software solution) including full product feature set, end to end support across multiple channels, documentation, pricing range etc.

Product Managers need to invest significantly in product marketing and positioning, pricing, operations, support, documentation in crossing the chasm. It requires a significant investment in making the transition and this is when the companies are looking for venture capital and additional funding.

Project Life Cycle

Project life cycle begins to the left of the Product Adoption cycle. This is because before customers can adopt the product, the product has to be built. Before you introduce the minimum viable product (MVP) in the market, the product manager has to write the requirements, use cases, think through the persona's and work with the development team to build the product.

A project life cycle is the process of planning, organizing, coordinating and governing of a project effectively to deliver it efficiently. The goal is to deliver the project on time, within cost with high quality.

A typical project life cycle is shown below:

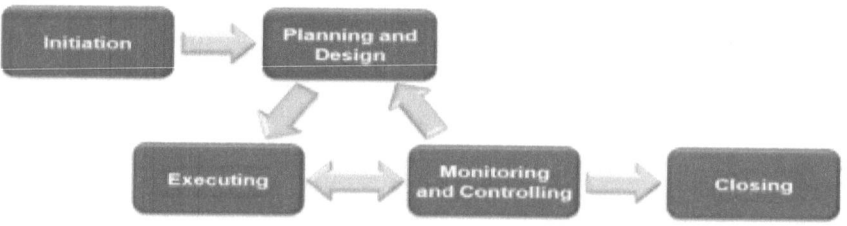

Source: https://en.m.wikipedia.org/wiki/Project_management

Initiation or Ideation: As a product manager, this is when the idea of the product and its feature set is being conceived. What is the problem you are solving?

Planning and Design: Here the product manager is writing the requirements, working with the teams to ensure they understand the requirements, working with the UX team on the experience of the product.

Execution: Here the Product Manager is clarifying the requirements, answering any questions, participating in the demos and providing feedback. The project manager has a more significant role here, ensuring the different roadblocks are cleared, teams are aligned, dependencies are clear etc.

Monitoring and Controlling: This as well is a Project Manager led phase, ensuring any progress towards the timelines, testing is on track, documentation is being provided and if any roadblocks, ensure they are overcome.

Closing/Launch: While this is closing the project, this is the launch of the product. Ensure testing is completed on the live product, support (war room or remote) is in place, review any issues identified post launch and develop a plan to resolve. Product Manager needs to ensure marketing activities are launched, sales teams are aware of the launch activities etc.

As the Project Life Cycle activities need to happen before the product adoption phase, this is where we will start, beginning with ideation and review the activities of a product manager at each stage of the product.

CHAPTER 2: IDEATION

The ideation phase is when the product idea is being conceived. Depending on your organization, role etc., this might take many forms. You may have (be given) a problem statement, or you might be the innovation prime looking for a problem to solve. The podcast by Steven Johnson "Where good ideas come from", is a must watch https://youtu.be/NugRZGDbPFU

In the Ideation or Initiation phase, the product manager is focused on building the following:
- Ideation
  - Product Vision,
  - Product Strategy,
  - Objectives,
  - Roadmap

Product Vision

Product vision is the "North Star" for your product - what is the end goal you would ideally like to achieve. A product vision statement should be ambitious and timeless. An example of a product vision could be simple "**Create #1 social gaming platform**". It communicates the goal, indicates how (gaming app), target (social gamers) - it allows the rest of the organization to rally behind the vision. Everybody from developers, testers, marketing can make decisions that ensure your product is moving in the direction of your North Star. We will refer back to this vision statement often.

The product vision statement should be supportive of your organization visions statement. As product manager you may not have much influence on the organization vision (hopefully you are aligned and believe it, if not find another job!), you inherit it.

Examples of organizational vision statement are:

Amazon:

"Our vision is to be earth's most customer centric company; to build a place where people can come to find and discover anything they might want to buy online."

Patagonia:

"Build the best product, cause no unnecessary harm, use business to inspire and implement solutions to the environmental crisis."

Ikea:

"At Ikea, our vision is to create a better everyday life for the many people. Our business idea supports this vision by offering a wide range of well-designed, functional home furnishing products at prices so low that as many people as possible will be able to afford them."

Having a vision statement enables everybody to be empowered to make decisions - the criteria is simple, how does this take us closer to the North Star?

This is extremely critical - if you are a small startup or working as product manager at a large organization, you will need a team to succeed. You need the team to be able to make rapid decisions without having to come back to you every time, which is possible only if they are aligned with your product vision.

If you find yourself going back and changing decisions your team members have made, you have a lack of alignment on the vision and to be successful that lack of alignment will need to be corrected.

How do you help your team achieve that alignment or "product vision"? Having a well communicated and clear product strategy, helps guide the team.

Product Strategy

Product strategy indicates what you are going to work on over the next three years to achieve your product vision. Strategy indicates as an organization what you are going to work on to achieve your goals.

With the vision of creating a "#1 social gaming platform", a strategy to achieve that would be as follows:

	1H'Y1	2H'Y1	Y2	Y3
Platform	• Hire developers to build generic platform. • Build and launch games	• Develop capability to have 3rd parties publish games • Setup monetization mechanism	• Enhance ease of developing and publishing games • Improve social interaction	• Develop VR/AR capability
Marketing		• Market games	• Market to 3rd party game developers	• Win award for platform

The strategy gives some level of detail for year 1 (Y1), a very broad description of what needs to be done in Y2 and Y3. This should be a living document and reviewed often. In larger organizations the strategy would involve Sales strategy, operations strategy etc. While you may have an extremely detailed strategy document you need to boil it down to a couple bullet points that the organization can rally behind.

The product strategy leads to the question of how are we going to achieve this? We need a roadmap to help us work on executing the strategy.

Product Roadmap

A product roadmap is a view of what we need to execute on to achieve our strategic goals. In an agile development environment this would be the backlog, in a hybrid environment which is a combination of waterfall and agile you would have a roadmap and backlog and specific points where the development teams have to integrate with each other's code.

The roadmap is specific to what needs to be developed and is leveraged to identify the resources required to support this effort, the cost allocation and timelines for when specific features would be delivered.

Continuing the above theme of creating the #1 social gaming platform, the roadmap may look like this:

Q1	Q2	Q3	Q4
• Develop library to build avatars • Develop library to allocate resources • Develop library to control movement • Develop platform for developers to build games	• Build library to enable social interactions • Build library to purchase resources • Build library to create bots to play against humans • Enable platform to publish games	• Develop library for players to create profiles • Support association of profiles to games • Create recommendation engine for games	• Scale the platform to support 1M games • Scale the platform to support 10K games

While the above is an example, it provides key attributes of a roadmap:

1. Timelines in which specific features need to be built
2. For each period, provides a high level description of the feature

This is combined with detailed (or at least high level) requirements which would enable the development team to provide cost as well as confirm the listed features can likely be developed in the timeline.

Teams working in an agile environment will have a backlog and start grooming the requirements at this stage.

The focus should be on developing a minimum viable product (MVP) that can be tested in the market. The question is how do you determine what is the boundary of an MVP?

CHAPTER 3: VALIDATION

Validation is key in ensuring the product being developed is in line with the expectations of the target customer and they will pay for it.

This is done by focusing efforts on developing the minimum feature set and testing the product with customers as early as possible. To be able to define the minimum viable product (MVP), you will require to do specific research as well have a good idea of what the competitive products (or alternatives to your product are).

In the Validation Phase, the product manager is focused on the following activities:
- Validation
  - MVP,
  - Competitive Analysis,
  - Market Research

Minimum Viable Product

A Minimum Viable Product (MVP) is a product that lets you test the core problem you are trying to solve with the least amount of features. It is aimed at small subset of customers (early adopters)

The purpose of building an MVP is to be able to test a product hypothesis while investing a minimal set of resources. The key drivers of building an MVP are:

- Accelerate learnings and get feedback from the early adopters.
- Reduce wasted engineering hours by only building features that are supported and based on real feedback from the early adopters.
- Get the product to early customers as soon as possible
- If it is a new startup, build your brand quickly

The Key MVP elements include:

- **Functionality** – the set of features must deliver clear value to the user,
- **Design** – the design of the MVP must be up to the highest industry standard,
- **Reliability** – While early adopters are usually forgiving, you should have a good production quality standard.
- **Usability** – the MVP must be relatively easy to use and intuitive (you can assume early adopters will research and be technically savvy).

As you are defining your MVP, you need to have a good understanding of the expectations of the customers. This is done by performing market research.

Market Research

You can perform market research ahead of developing the MVP and then go back and further validate once you have built the MVP. Your market research should include specific product specific research (which features, use cases etc.) as well as industry research.

In the following sections, we will cover:
- Product Research
- Industry Research

Product Research

Prior to MVP Development

Ahead of spending dollars on building an MVP, you can leverage multiple forms of research to get a good idea of what the customers' expectations are, what are the current alternatives to solving the problem your product solves, how and where would the customer use your product. The following techniques can be leveraged ahead of developing the MVP:

- **Interview**: Interview potential customers who might use your product, ask them detailed questions around the problem you are solving. How do they solve that problem today? What are the alternative solutions? What does it cost? What do they not like about the current solution? The advantage of interviews is you can ask follow up questions, clarifying questions etc. The disadvantage is this method does not scale and is not conducive to being quantified.
- **Survey**: You can perform a survey to get an understanding of how your potential customers perceive the problem you are trying to solve. With a survey you need to ensure you are not asking leading questions. Survey (unlike interviews) is not conducive to open ended questions. The big advantage of leveraging surveys is on a small budget you can reach a large audience and further the responses can be quantified, analyzed for patterns, correlation factors can be identified, sensitivity analysis can be performed etc.
- **Service Design**: Service Design is a much deeper form of interview. Invite a select few potential customers (based on the persona's you have identified), and spend a couple hours (or days, depending on your budget) with the customer. Usually you are paying for the customer's time

as this is time intensive. In this form you can walk the customer through your on boarding process (for example using sticky notes for each step), low fidelity mockup of your screens (PowerPoint or even hand drawn screens on paper) etc. This provides a much deeper understanding of what resonates with a customer and what did not work with the customer etc.

Post MVP Availability

During the MVP development the product manager (or product owner) acts as the voice of the customer. Once you have a working MVP, get friendly customers to give the product a try.

MVP Demonstration: During the MVP development, at meaningful points you might want to demonstrate the product to a customer to get feedback. You are typically not allowing the customer to use it (as many flows may still be under development), only showing the customer flows that are completed and getting feedback.

MVP Trial: When the MVP is completed, you can get feedback on the product from the early adopters. The trial provides an opportunity to see how the product would be used by real customers (outside of the lab environment), which features are used vs. not used, identify any technical issues etc., and these insights are invaluable ahead of product launch.

Industry Research

Along with the product research, the product manager needs to develop a good understanding of the market. This is required to be able to correctly position the product in the market, make pricing decisions and finally how the distribution (and support) would be done. This is the standard 4Ps of marketing, which the product manager needs to lead.

Competitive Analysis

A competitive advantage is an advantage over competitors gained by offering higher value, either by means of lowering price or by providing higher benefits and service that justifies greater price.

Porter suggested four "generic" business strategies that could be adopted in order to gain competitive advantage. The strategies relate to the extent to which the scope of a business' activities are narrow versus broad and the extent to which a business seeks to differentiate its products.

The strategies that Porter suggested are appropriate to seek competitive advantage are summarized in the figure below:

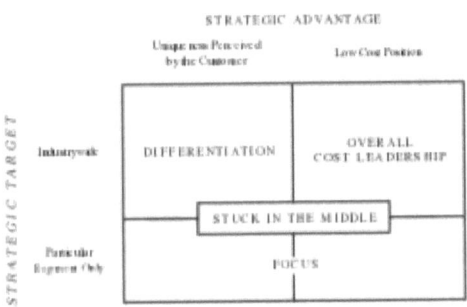

Source: Wikipedia

Cost Leadership: If the firm is targeting customers in most or all segments of an industry based on offering the lowest price, it is following a cost leadership strategy. Walmart is a good example of this strategy.

Differentiation Strategy: Target customer segment on attributes other than price (e.g., Higher product quality to command a higher price) it is differentiation. For example Apple's products.

Focus strategy – Firm focus on one or a few segments of customers. An example is Costco.

You have various tools that can be leveraged for this:
1. SWOT Analysis
2. Porter's Five Forces
3. PESTEL Analysis

Swot Analysis

SWOT Analysis is a tool Product Managers can use at various points. To perform the competitive analysis of a company or product or even a feature. In the current context we are using it for Competitive Analysis. Identify the strength, weakness, opportunities and threats of the competitor.

The trick is in documenting this information over time. Sources where the product manager is listening and keeping track of this information are
1. Press releases, white paper, collateral - published by the competitor.
2. Quarterly and annual reports of a public company.
3. Sales team - your sales team has a lot of information on the competitor, speak to all your sales primes and they will provide golden nuggets that might not be public.

4. Ex-sales of the competitor: Ex-employees of the company can give you a lot of information, while it might be dated it tells you about the personalities involved, their management style
5. Job posting - Look at the job postings of the competitor, if they are venturing into a new product or new technology they will hire from outside.

Ensure your SWOT analysis includes not just product, expand it to include financial situation, regulator or legal issues, people strength (well-connected board for example) etc.

Porter's Five Forces

Porter's five forces provides a framework for performing competitive analysis of a business, which can also be used to perform the competitive analysis of a product.

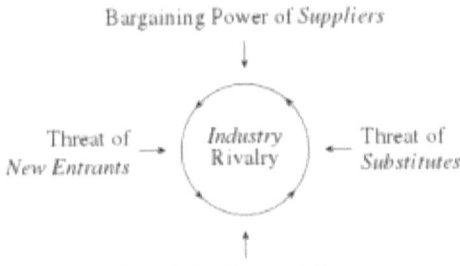

Source: Wikipedia

Threat of New Entrants: This is to analyze how easy it would be for a new entrant to enter the market. For example banking or utilities the threat of new entrants is low vs. social gaming the threat of new entrants is very high.

Threat of substitutes: What is the substitute for your product (including do-nothing)? For example, the threat of substitutes for Netflix was low in the 2010s, but in the last few years Disney+, HBO+, Crave, Hotstar and a number of new substitutes have entered the market.

Bargaining Power of suppliers: Your product might depend on suppliers providing raw materials (for example Apple is dependent on Foxconn for manufacturing), Amazon on courier and postal service for delivery.

Bargaining power of Buyers: What are the options the buyer has? If the buyer has a number of equally good options, the buyer has a lot of power vs. if the buyer has limited choice they have low bargaining power. For example by limiting iTunes to Apple products, Apple has control over it with essentially the customer having no choice but to buy music from Apple.

Product Managers should use the Porter's five forces framework when analyzing the market as a whole. Should the organization launch a product into an adjacent market - what are the dynamics of that market?

Pestel Analysis

PEST analysis (political, economic, socio-cultural and technological) describes a framework of macro-environmental factors used in the environmental scanning component of strategic management. It is part of an external analysis when conducting a strategic analysis or doing market research, and gives an overview of the different macro-environmental factors to be taken into consideration. It is a strategic tool for understanding market growth or decline, business position, potential and direction for operations.

Once you have completed the validation stage, a product manager needs to plan for the product launch. This is the stage when the most significant capital spend will happen, to ensure success a lot of planning needs to be completed ahead of entering the development stage.

CHAPTER 4: PLANNING

During the planning stage, the product manager is preparing to scale the product. At this stage you have validated the product with the early adopters & innovators (crossing the chasm) and scaling for the "early majority" or "growth" phase of the product.

During the planning phase product manager completes the following:

- Business Model,
- Business Case,
- Product Requirements (Waterfall, Agile),
- Feature Prioritization,
- Roadmap,
- Pricing,
- Forecasting,
- Stakeholder Management

While for each of the above you might have already worked on drafts, in the planning stage you are able to finalize each of the elements based on the learnings of working with innovators and early adopters.

Business Model

A good business model answers Peter Drucker's age-old questions, 'Who is the customer? And what does the customer value?' It also answers the fundamental questions every product manager must ask: How do we make money from this product?

What is the underlying economic principle that explains how we can deliver value to customers at an appropriate cost, for which the customer is willing to pay?"

The business model identifies:

Target Customer: Who is the target customer? This is done by identifying personas of target customers, as well as highlighting demographics, target regions (countries) etc.

Monetization: How are you earning money from the product? For example for a social gaming platform you could earn money from In-game purchases, advertisements, pay for the app etc. B2B models could be based on license model, fixed pricing, combination of fixed minimum pricing and license based on growth etc.

Addressable Market Size:

Here you are answering the question, is this space worth getting into (or if you already are, what is the expected growth). Assuming you are getting into this space, you need to figure out the following:

1. Total Addressable Market Size (TAM): This is the total market size globally, i.e., number of customers that your product can be sold to and the total expected revenue from it.
2. Serviceable Addressable Market Size (SAM) : Given your competitor's are going to take a share, as well as you may not have sales globally but only in limited areas (and other corporate strategy limitations), what is the actual market that you can service?

3. Share of Market (SOM): Of the market that is now serviceable, what do you expect your organization can get?

The business model sets up which customers you are targeting, how will you monetize your product and how much market share can you expect, based on this you can develop the business case.

Business Case

Business case is usually done for three to five years. The basic essence is to ensure you are profitable over time.

A very simplistic example is below:

	Year 1	Year 2	Year 3	Total
Cost	$480,000	$130,000	$60,000	$670,000
Revenue	$120,000	$750,000	$1,130,000	$2,000,000
Cash Flow	($360,000)	$620,000	$1,070,000	

NPV: $1,143,807

To calculate the cost you need to get your development team(s) to work out the full cost of coding, testing and maintaining the product (account of full time employees, contractors etc.). The cost should include the 3rd party licenses, hardware, 3rd party vendor solutions included (if any) etc.

To calculate the revenues you need to have the sales team to generate a projection of sales, in line with the marketing efforts, discounting and pricing models that will be used etc. These can become very complex depending on how many SKU codes, discounting models etc.

Your organization may also look for the Internal Rate of Return (IRR) to ensure the profitability (and to compare with other product initiatives) to identify products with the best return on investments.

Product Requirements

Product requirement document (PRD) provides an overview of the purpose of the product and lists the detailed requirements of the product.

Having a detailed product requirements document ensures
- Clarity in scope of the product,
- Ability to develop good cost assessment for the development and testing of the product,
- Ability to commit to firm timelines based on the requirements

A good PRD will list all the functional and nonfunctional requirements of the product.

Functional Requirements: The functional requirements include how the product would be setup, used, covers the different personas and use cases.

Nonfunctional Requirements: The nonfunctional requirements cover the security, scalability, availability, revenue assurance, regulatory, privacy, legal requirements of the product.

The downside of writing a PRD, based on customer validation (earlier chapter) your requirements might change as you find new information. Unforeseen challenges arise throwing your cost, timeline assessment out. The alternative is using agile methodology where possible.

User Stories
In Agile, you write up the backlog which captures your requirements at a high level. You only groom the stories that will be developed in the upcoming sprint (usually two weeks of coding and testing).

The advantage of doing this
- You are focusing on what is already known

- You develop user stories that can be demonstrated (to the product owner or stakeholders)
- As new information is made available, you can easily adapt.

The downside of Agile methodology is you cannot provide a fixed timeline of delivery, this is mitigated by having frequent demos and not having a firm cost, this is mitigated by knowing the velocity of development and cost of each sprint, you can determine how much you want to invest. In Agile you want to develop the most important features first, this is done by feature prioritization.

Feature Prioritization

As you have limited time, money you always need to prioritize your most important features to take to market. Develop the Minimum viable product that allows the customer to test your product. This is also discussed in the Minimum Viable Product section earlier in the book.

In order to develop an unbiased mechanism to prioritize features, you may have one or more of the following items against which you would prioritize:

- Strategic Importance
- Revenue
- Effort
- Complexity
- Time to Market
- Theme

Let's dig a little deeper into each of these.

Strategic Importance

Strategic Importance reflects the importance of a particular feature, where strategic importance is loosely defined as alignment with the organizational strategic goals, or importance to key sponsor or key customer.

Alignment with the organization goal is obviously important. For example if the goal of the organization is to increase digital adoption and your roadmap feature does not have any significant enhancement to increase digital adoption, you are likely not going to get much support from the executives. This will result in your roadmap being heavily debated as it does not align with the key goals of the organization.

Similarly if a flagship customer's (typical in B2B scenario) desired features (read customization) is not included in the roadmap and this will result in the customer not taking the update, head of Sales is not going to support the product roadmap.

Many product Managers struggle with wading through the internal politics and how to demonstrate the value of a feature. Product Managers struggle with getting alignment on should a particular feature be implemented or not? Depending on if an internal stakeholder wants this feature (or not!). Leveraging "Strategic Importance" allows you to highlight (or deprioritize) the feature.

Revenue

Revenue is a straight reflection of the additional revenue this feature is going to bring in. Features that are going to bring in additional revenue typically are prioritized high as they will build the business case for building the product. These features typically solve a pain point or problem for the customer and so help the customer make the business case for the upgrade (or purchase).

Sales teams look for these features in a roadmap, and if your roadmap is lite on these features you will not have their support.

Effort

Effort reflects the work that needs to be done to develop the feature. This is typically translated in the person-day(s) effort, which can then result in a dollar value associated with the effort. The conversion of the person-day effort to a dollar value is based on the loaded labor cost used by your organization (or an industry specific average).

Complexity

Complexity reflects how complex that specific feature is to develop. This is usually a reflection of
- How many teams are involved in building this feature?
- How many systems are impacted?
- How clearly is the feature understood? If unclear, it is classified as complex until you can spend more time assessing it in a deeper fashion.

Less complex features usually are very well understood, impacting only a small number of teams and systems. While very complex features will impact a large number of teams and systems. You need to ensure you have included the cost from all of the teams and systems including those that might only be required to support from a testing perspective.

Time To Market

Time to market in this context is "how long does it take me to take this feature to market"? It is also reflected in the effort and complexity elements. The reason to call it out separately is sometimes you have features which have high effort and are complex, yet would have got prioritized based on the revenue potential. But if because of timelines, that revenue would only come in 18 months later for example (due to the effort and complexity), we might have other features that can be prioritized and brought to market earlier.

Theme

You can have a theme for your roadmap, and features that align with that theme are automatically prioritized. Typical themes may be Digital Adoption, Customer Effort Reduction, Security Enhancements, and Privacy Enhancements etc.

This allows you to group low priority features bundle them up and together may have a higher priority as well as become more impactful for the customer.

These are some examples of elements you can use to prioritize your features, next you have to build the weighted prioritization matrix to help you systematically prioritize these features.

Weighted Prioritization Matrix

A Weighted Prioritization Matrix takes the prioritization criteria from above and associates a weight to it. This allows the

Product Manager to control the criteria and how they reflect into the roadmap. It also allows you to explain to the organization the thought process behind the roadmap.

For each of the elements you provide a scale, let's say 1 to 5 where 5 signifies high strategic importance vs. 1 signifies the lowest level. Usually use only 3 elements (like 1, 3, 5), this allows for clearer demarcation and clarity on high, medium or low.

An example of Weighted Prioritization Matrix using the elements identified above is shown below:

	Strategic Importance	Revenue	Complexity	Theme	Priority Score
Weightage	35%	20%	10%	25%	
Feature A	5	5	3	1	3.3
Feature B	3	1	3	5	2.8
Feature C	1	3	5	1	1.7

In the above Table Feature A has the highest priority score vs Feature C has the lowest priority score.

Top Right Prioritization

Another mechanism to prioritize features is to select two priorities for Example Revenue and Strategic Importance and plot the features with these two elements as axis.

Top Right Priority

This allows you to show elements that have high Revenue and are strategically important to the organization at the top right. This mechanism is not as systematic, but can be done quite rapidly, especially if your organization is focused on one or two specific goals.

At the end of this prioritization activity, you now have a list of features and a timeline of when these can be delivered. Pulling the list of prioritized features and mapping into a timeline provides the roadmap.

Roadmap

Product Roadmap serves as a document to align the organization around a detailed set of features that will be delivered. The roadmap serves a number of functions, a product manager has to manage multiple roadmap (distinct roadmaps, aimed at different audiences), manager versions of the roadmap to ensure it is a living document and adapts as elements change, ensure that they can tell the story how of the roadmap evolved over time and the basis for the various decisions made along the way. Wow, that is a lot to cover. Let's first break down the different types of roadmaps.

Types of Roadmaps

As stated you have to manage different types of roadmap (note this is not just a different version, it is a distinctly different type of roadmap). The different types of roadmaps that a product manager needs to manage are

- Visionary Roadmap
- Based on Audience
- Based on Timeframe
- Based on Themes

These roadmaps are just different views of the core roadmap. Product Manager should focus most time on managing this core roadmap that has a detailed list of all the features. Depending on the audience, theme, timeframe you just use the appropriate view of the core roadmap.

An example of a detailed roadmap is below.

Detailed Roadmap

Q1'20	Q2'20	Q3'20	Q4'20
• Build 6 characters of game • Build 12 buildings • Build ability to upgrade building • Build ability to upgrade characters • Build logic of collecting resources gems and gold • Build ability to purchase upgrades • Build ability to provide bonus offers • Build on both Android and iOS • Build capability to play against AI • Build capability for AI based players	• Build additional 4 characters • Build additional 3 buildings • Build 1 Super Character • Build logic to purchase gems • Build ability to chat with other players • Build clans • Build ability to fight other human players • Support 400K concurrent gamers • Support 100K concurrent transactions • Fix operational issues	• Build additional 2 characters • Build 1 additional building • Build 2nd super character • Ability to design base • Ability to have 3 base configurations to select from • Ability to have Clan wars • Ability to automatically record games • Ability to view recorded games • Fix operational issues	• Build 3rd Super Character • Ability to upload games to Social Media • Ability to visit other bases • Build ability to have tiers of players • Scale the product to support 1M concurrent gamers • Fix operational issues

Now the same Roadmap can be used to build a visionary roadmap and that would be represented as follows:

Visionary Roadmap

Develop MVP Product Launch with Friendly Customer	Develop Operational Support Process Scale customer base	Automate Development Strategy
2020	**2021**	**2022**

Further the same roadmap may be shown at a C-Level Presentation as follows

C-Level Roadmap

Q1'20	Q2'20	Q3'20	Q4'20
• Build 18 characters and Buildings • Build ability to upgrade building & Characters • Build logic of collecting resources gems and gold • Build ability to purchase upgrades • Build on both Android and IOS • Build AI Capabilities to test game	• Build 7 additional characters & buildings • Build 1 Super Character • Build logic to purchase gems • Build ability to chat with other players • Build clans • Build ability to fight other human players	• Build 3 additional characters & building • Build 2nd super character • Ability to design different base configurations • Ability to have Clan wars • Game Recordings	• Build 3rd Super Character • Ability to upload games to Social Media • Build ability to have tens of players • Improve Scalability

The difference in the above roadmap is the level of detail. A product manager should be able to talk to each feature in the detailed roadmap in lots of detail (why is it useful, how does it help align with the strategy, how does it help in revenue/cost saving etc.)

Pricing

Now that you have your roadmap, you may identify some releases that go to market (if not all of them). You have worked out your business model (i.e., how are going to make money) and your target segment, you need to determine the actual pricing.

Few different methods to determine the price. The most common pricing strategies include

1. **Cost-plus pricing**: Most straight forward, simply add all your costs and add a mark-up.
2. **Competitive pricing**: In this strategy, you study the competitive pricing of existing products in the market and set a price based on what the competition charges. Add a discount or additional value for features you do not have or have beyond what the competition has.
3. **Value-based pricing**: This strategy is based on how much the customer believes what your product is worth. This is the model used by Apple for example.
4. **Price skimming**: In this strategy you set a high price and lower it as the market evolves. This is typically done when you have a new innovative product in the market, as the competition catches up you lower the price.
5. **Penetration pricing**: In this strategy you set a low price to enter a competitive market and raise it later. This is typically done when you are entering an already competitive market and trying to build your market share.

For most B2B software products, I am a big fan of value based pricing. To maximize the price you need to be aware of

- **Brand Value**: What is the perception of your brand? Are you able to demand a premium over the market price?

- **Product Value**: What is the cost to the customer organization of not having your product? How does your product improve the current process? For example if your product can save 30 seconds of every call at a call center, and the call center processes a million calls a day, each with an average cost of $10 per call lasting 10 minutes, You save them $0.5M/day. That is the value you are adding to the organization.
- **Revenue share**: If you are confident of the value and it is easily measurable, you could enter a revenue share model with the customer. Typically structured a minimum up-front cost (usually cost + markup) and then additional pricing based on a % share of the benefits gained by the customer.

Note - Value based pricing can only be applied if you are entering a blue-ocean (minimal competition) or if your brand value can support it.

Forecasting

Forecasting is critical, as the success of your product depends on the accuracy of the sales forecast (at the above price points).

Product Manager needs to be close to the sales team, have a deep understanding of the sales funnel and the associated revenue generation forecast. Product Managers should be aware of the criteria to move a customer along the funnel.

Awareness: This is the lead generation, making the potential customers know about your product, organizations etc.

Discovery: Qualification stage of the product, does it meet the customer's needs? Any unique requirements, customization required to deploy the product?

Quote: What is the price that should be quoted, including the cost of any unique customizations, deployment, scale that needs to be supported? Any discounts that need to be provided?

Purchase: Once the product is purchased, ensure product deployment goes smoothly. The right hardware and resources to deploy the hardware/software are on site, and ensure to meet the launch timelines of the customer.

Loyalty: Product Manager needs to ensure that the customer is satisfied with the product, any gaps/issues are corrected in a timely manner and as the needs of the customer (or market) evolve, and your product roadmap keeps up with those requirements ensuring further upgrade (sales).

Stakeholder Management

It is a critical skill for a product manager to have good stakeholder relationships. Your goal when presenting the roadmap, is to have it socialized and approved individually with the c-level primes and approved. You need to have addressed (or be prepared) to address any concern from the stakeholder.

Who are the stakeholders?

It is critical to answer the following questions as you are identifying your stakeholders:
- Who are the C-level primes in the room that actually control the funding and resourcing?
- Who is critically impacted by this roadmap?
- Do you have the support from the sales VP? Marketing VP?
- Do you have support from your team C-Level?

Socialize your roadmap

For each of the C-Levels you identify, you need to work with primes in that team and ensure you have incorporated their requirements, feedback into the roadmap. Once the roadmap is near final, review it with the director level (either individually or have a session with key directors) and review the roadmap.

The management level would like much more detail in-terms of their individual areas. For example, the development team will be concerned with the resourcing, accuracy of cost estimates and timelines. Sales team will be concerned about how this updated product could be sold, what are the benefits, what is the upgrade price, who will be the first upgrade customer etc. Marketing team will be concerned with what are the new capabilities and how can they be marketed, does it expand the target market, does it require different messages for different segments etc.

As you have walked through and answered each of these questions, the key question towards the end should be can we walk the individual c-level of the team through the roadmap. Either you walk the c-level through the roadmap or have the team prime walk the c-level.

An example of this is you walk the Sales VP through the roadmap, followed by a detailed analysis of which sales opportunities this opens up, what the revenue potential look likes, what is committed in the business case. Similarly with a Marketing VP you would walk them through the roadmap and then the marketing prime walks through the go-to-market plan, messaging, timelines, costs etc.

This is a critical step as this buys the support from the c-level prime, so when you present your roadmap for approval you have support from all the stakeholders.

As you can see this does not happen overnight, this requires a lot of planning, socializing, updating your roadmap based on feedback etc. Getting alignment is extremely important to the success of the product.

Now that you have the alignment and approval of the c-level, you have to deliver on the commitments. At this stage a Product Manager has to shift gears into an execution mode, ideally with the help of a strong project manager or in many instances the product manager has to play the role of a project manager (which I do not support).

CHAPTER 5: EXECUTION

The execution phase is critical, because as the product manager you have made commitment to the leadership on delivering the product and the associated benefits.

To successfully bring in the benefits, you need to deliver the product roadmap at cost, in the timelines committed, support the marketing team in advertising and the sales team in closing the sales.

Before you can market and sell, you need to deliver the product. To be able to deliver at cost and on time, you need the support of a strong project manager, or sharpen your project management skills.

Kick-Off

Once you have got the approval from the C-level team on your roadmap, you need to kick off the project to deliver your next release. A successful kick-off requires the following:

- Goal,
- Scope,
- Resourcing (core team),
- RACI
- Governance and
- Success Criteria

Goal

What is the goal of the project? It is to deliver certain core capability or the next release of your roadmap? Is it to gain certain new customers?

It is critical you have a specific goal and everybody on the project core team is clear on the goal. The goal should be a sentence or two, very crisp and focused.

Scope

What is in scope of the project? List the different features that need to be delivered at a high level (this is not a requirements document, but a broad statement of the scope of the project). This would include the features, type of customers supported, sub-brands supported, channels supported etc.

Just as important as what is in-scope, is a list of elements that are out of scope. For example which sub-brands are out of scope, which types of customers will not be supported, any channels that will not be supported in this release should be documented in the kick off deck.

The reason this is critical is it ensures, based on this high level scope which resources or team members we need support from.

Resourcing

Based on the above scope, now you can identify which core team members you require. You need the development primes from the development team, testing primes, support from channels (retail, digital, dealers or however you are planning to sell/support your product), marketing prime etc. This team is your core team and you need to ensure you have dedicated support from this team.

You may also have other team members who are not part of the core team, these are usually the ones that only need to be informed about your product or approve your product launch but do not need to be in the day-to-day details of the project. This usually includes Privacy, Security, Legal, Regulatory, revenue assurance, fraud etc.

To make sure expectations are clear on the roles and responsibilities of each member of the team, it is best to have a RACI (or similar documentation).

Raci

RACI is an acronym derived from the four key responsibilities most typically used: responsible, accountable, consulted, and informed. It is used for clarifying and defining roles and responsibilities in cross-functional or departmental projects and processes.

- Responsible: A role that is "Responsible" for completing the task or deliverable.
- Accountable: A role that is "Accountable" has the final authority or accountability for the task's completion.
- Consulted: A role that is "Consulted" is an adviser to a task.
- Informed: A role that is "Informed" is kept up to date on task completion. This is critical as many of the leadership roles will fall in this category and you will require their support when you hit a roadblock.

An example of a RACI chart typically looks like this (only an illustration):

	Role 1	Role 2	Role 3	Role 4
Project Planning	A	R	I	C
Requirements	C	C	C	A
User Experience	C	C	I	A
Privacy Approval	I	I	A	C
Security Approval	I	I	A	C
QA	I	A	I	C
End User Acceptance	I	I	A	C

Some commons best practices on coming up with a RACI chart:
- Avoid using names at the top of the columns, use the team/group names or roles. As during the life of the project team

members will change.

- Assign only one Accountable per task
- Ensure Accountable assignees have the authority to ensure the task is complete
- During the life of the project, review the RACI multiples times, especially if it is unclear who should be doing a task
- Make sure during kick-off everybody agrees to their role in the RACI. This is critical, as your project success depends on it.

Governance Structure

The Product Manager needs to set expectations of how the project will be governed. This includes what are the regular meetings (how will you keep all the team members on the same page), does it include a weekly core call? Who are the required members who will need to attend every week?

How will you store the documentation associated with the project? How will requirements be captured (format, tool etc.)?

How will the leadership be kept informed of the progress and roadblocks as the project moves forward? Do you have bi-weekly meetings with the director? Do you have a formal steer-co forum that you will need to present the project at?

How will you keep the C-Level team informed of the project, do you bring it to a specific forum for review?

Will you be sending weekly project email updates and if so what is the format, who will be on it?

Capturing this information in the kick-off deck ensures all team members are aware of the governance process, and can ensure expectations with their leadership teams are set on how they will be informed of the project progress.

Success Criteria

During the kick off, giving the team visibility into what success looks like is important. The project team will find ways to be successful, if they know what success looks like. Have specific KPIs with Targets, threshold and stretch goals that are measurable, specific and time bound. Some KPIs for any project are on the variance on spend profile, timelines (including interim timelines of having requirements signed off, development complete etc.) and measure of post launch activities (tying it to your goals either revenue, customers using the product etc.)

At the very start gather all of the above information and have a formal kick off meeting. Ensure you have the primes from each team required including the non-core team members and walk through the entire deck, ensure you get alignment on each aspect of the kick off deck. If primes are missing ensure they are added and review the kick off deck with them.

Having a good kick off to your project, provides a strong foundation to ensure success of the project.

Governance

Governance is the process of how you will communicate and manage the changes in the project, risks associated with the project etc.

Governance essentially is ensuring you have a plan and process to communicate with the following:

- Core team,
- Stakeholder,
- Sponsor,
- C-Level

Core Team

During kick-off of the project you have identified the core team members that are required to ensure success of the product. As part of the governance process you should have a recurring schedule of when you will meet as a core team (ideally weekly), have a clear distribution list of the core teams and ideally messaging (slack, hangouts etc.) group for this team.

While the weekly core team meetings likely are attended by all the team members, most of "inform" roles in the RACI might just choose to be part of email distribution.

This ensures you keep the working team on the same page as the project runs into challenges, changes, make assumptions etc.

Stakeholder

I refer to the manager/directors of the core team members as the stakeholders. This is the group you would most likely escalate to when you run into people challenges, significant change in assumptions, new scope etc.

The typical cadence of meeting with the stakeholder is by having a Stakeholder Steerco bi-weekly.

In some organizations I have seen "escalation" is a feared word, because it implies something is not going well. By having a steerco every two weeks you keep the management informed of the changes and ask for help as soon as the issue is identified.

Sponsor

You should have identified your project sponsor during the kick off process. The sponsor is typically a C-Level executive who will provide you any cross functional support required from the other teams. As well in many large organizations teams may not have visibility into what is happening in other parts of the organization, which a C-level executive would have been able to get.

The role of the C-level executive is both to be a champion of the initiative as well as be the prime looking beyond the "silo" to see how other projects can impact this project.

The product and project managers should connect with the sponsor at least once a month on a regular basis.

C-Level

Organizations usually have a regular cadence that they meet with and usually projects would have a criteria (or gate) that would dictate when they present to the c-level.

To be able to present to the c-level, you need to ensure that your core team has contributed to the deck, get sign-off from the stakeholder and finally review it ahead of time with your c-level.

Doing this above is critical as it does a few things:
- Ensures all risks, perspectives are captured. If any is missed that director/stakeholder will have to speak up (as they did not bring it up earlier).
- Your sponsor can guide you the kind of questions that will be asked,
- It ensures you have lots of support in the room when you present

When you see projects that are performing smoothly (even when they have issues and delays), study their governance model it will be very similar to the above structure.

Trade-Offs

The Product and Project manager have to work together on the trade-offs. The project manager's role is to determine what the options are, usually you have to work with four levers - Scope, Cost, Quality and Time.

For example, if the team is running out of time, you can add more resources and this would increase cost, or you could compromise on the quality (reducing the amount of testing for example).

Alternatively, if additional scope has been identified, you can slip your timeline to accommodate this scope, add more resources (cost) to the project to meet the scope and time or you can compromise on the quality.

While the project manager comes up with the options, the product manager has a strong influence on the recommendation, for example may be the additional scope can be pushed to the next release, at the additional cost the business case breaks, of course lowering quality would usually not be acceptable.

Once you have a recommendation, you should run that by the core team and ensure everybody is aligned as well as present to your stakeholder and get sign off on the trade-off made.

Agile Development

To govern an agile team you would have the scrum planning, daily standup, demos and retrospectives.

If 100% of your development is being done by one agile team, it makes life easier. The Project Manager (in this case might be the scrum master) can manage the development as well as coordinate with marketing, operations, sales etc.

Agile And Waterfall

In many instances only part of the development is agile and the remainder is waterfall. In this case you may have a scrum master managing agile development, another project manager (or multiple project managers) managing waterfall development.

As the project manager responsible for the project, your role would be to leverage the governance structure you have put in place to hide the complexity of multiple project managers and plans and bring the big picture forward.

Product Managers will need to choose which meetings to attend, depending on the % of development being agile you should allocate the required time in ensuring the stories are groomed and attend the demos etc.

Provide the waterfall requirements, ensure they are understood, identify points of dependency between the two methodologies and ideally be able to abstract or remove those dependencies with the support of your developers (using stub APIs for example).

Unit Testing

This is the phase when you are testing individual functionality. You can isolate the buy flow and test it, test the different basic features etc.

As this is the first round of testing, you can expect a number of issues to be raised. Project manager's role is to prioritize the issues by severity and track the timelines for fixes.

Severity Levels

Organizations typically have standardized severity levels, if not the project manager should define them at the start of the project.

For example, a simple severity criteria definition could be as follows:

Severity Level	Description
S1	Issues that prevent the launch of the product. Customers cannot purchase or use the product as intended.
S2	Most customers will see this issue in normal usage.
S3	Very few customers would see this issue in normal usage. These are issues in how the product behaves in corner cases.

You can formalize the severity levels by having specific % of customers seeing the issues, or have more levels etc. depending on your organization.

Your kick off deck should have identified the success criteria for example "Zero S1 issues and 2 or less S2 issues" would be acceptable.

Typically these severity levels and launch criteria are not product specific rather the organization has a standard to which you need to comply. Irrespective of how they are defined, having them defined and everybody agreeing to them ensure the team is working towards one goal.

Multiple Iterations

As issues are identified and resolved, you need to ensure you have not broken something else. Typically a project manager will plan for a couple iterations of fixes and testing to ensure the quality of the product is at a level to move to the next phase.

Friendly Testing

Once unit testing is completed, you want to test the product in the real world. The first real world testing should be done with "Friendlies", who would be happy to give you feedback on every aspect of the product.

These can be employees (outside of the core team), or friends

& family who understand that you are looking for feedback. No point if they are nice and just say it was working.

Depending on your scale you can do this with a handful of customers or hundreds, you would likely need at least 20+ to get a decent feedback.

Project Manager should ensure that the development team is tracking the usage patterns, noticing issues (latency, click rates etc.). Product Managers should ensure these teams have the right tools to capture and support customers, so when in the real world a customer see's an issue the backend team is capable to see it as well and ideally resolve quickly.

Product Managers should have interviews with the participants to get more in-depth feedback. In the interview you should cover:
- How was the purchase flow?
- How long did it take to make the purchase? Did they get stuck in any place? Were the instructions clear? Did they have the information that was required to sign up for the product?
- How easy was it to set up the product? Or how easy was it to use the product?
- Did it meet the core expectations?
- What are the opportunities for improvement?

Assuming the feedback is positive, you move ahead with launch. If it is not positive you take these back to the developers, iterate to make the improvements.

Before moving to the launch, you would have noticed some overlap in the roles & responsibilities of a Product Manager in the execution phase.

Project Vs. Product Manager Responsibilities

In the planning phase, it is clear what the product manager role is.

It is about identifying the problem statement to solve, customer personas, validating the idea, building the business case etc.

After launch, the product manager will work closely with marketing, sales and operations teams.

It is during the execution phase that the overlap between product and project manager roles, that causes some confusion (and sometimes strife):

Stage	Product Manager	Project Manager
Planning	Problem Statement, Persona, Business case, Validation	Not assigned yet
Kick-Off	Present the Problem Statement and high level Scope	Organize the kick off deck, core team, ensure resourcing, funding in place. High level Project plan.
Requirements	Write the requirements and ensure all teams build solution to meet requirements	Organize the reviews, ensure all comments addressed. Changes in resourcing, funding etc. are addressed. Firm and detailed project plan.
Development	Answer any clarification questions about requirements or scope. Attend demos for Agile and help in grooming stories. Work on the next release persona, use case, business case etc.	Track project dependencies. Run the core team and governance meetings. Ensure timeline and budget are being met.
Testing	Sign-off on user level testing. Continue working on the next release persona, use case, business case etc.	Ensure unit testing and friendly testing dates are met. Any issues resolved and retested. Continue Core, Governance meetings.
Launch (will address in depth in next	Ensure marketing collateral and plans are ready, sales enablement documents are	Ensure launch criteria is met. Have a Go/No-Go meeting as part of your core and governance

section)	ready.	meetings.
Post Launch	Ensure marketing and sales activities are happening. Track KPIs, results and review high priority issues.	Ensure any post launch issues are resolved.

Typically project managers move on to another project or they go back into the execution phase of the next release.

The Product Manager continues supporting the current product release and tracks the marketing activities (success rates etc.) and sales activities (key customers in B2B scenarios, conferences etc.).

CHAPTER 6: LAUNCH AND MARKETING

As you approach launch, you have two key streams that need to be supported. The two stream of activities are
- Marketing
- Testing

Marketing on the day of launch includes a number of activities that need to be done once the product is live, you need to ensure these are completed and any issues are resolved.

Testing immediately after launch is to ensure everything works well in the production environment. All the purchase flows are working (digital or retail), product works well in production (end to end testing) etc.

To ensure you are prepared for launch, you need to go through the launch readiness criteria.

Launch Readiness

Built your product launch readiness checklist, with your core team. Typically the launch readiness checklist would cover the following:

- Is the product ready to launch - Is all the testing done. What is the severity of any of the issues outstanding and can we launch with these outstanding issues?
- Is the support team ready to support the product post launch? Do you have the process documented for support issues?
- Are all the marketing activities for the day of launch ready to go?
- Is the digital team ready to enable the product and support pages?
- Is the inventory in stock, SKUs codes in the system etc?
- Is the team ready to perform end to end testing in production? Who is signing off on the testing?
- Is the call center team ready to receive support calls? Have they had the right training to support the product?

Your organization might have other attributes, essentially your checklist should have a comprehensive list of things that are required for successful launch of your product.

Launch Go/No-Go

Once you have your launch readiness criteria in place, you should have a launch go/no-go meeting. Like the kick off meeting at the start of the project, the Launch Go/No-Go is a critical meeting.

You should have representatives from the leadership of each of the key teams involved in the product launch at this meeting. You are asking them to sign off on the launch plans.

At this meeting you review each of the launch readiness criteria from above and ask for approval to launch.

The function of this meeting is to ensure all teams are aware and leadership signs off that they have approved the launch.

Launch Day

On the launch day (or night), you kick off the launch activities, followed by the marketing activities.

Launch Activities starts with the development team launching the new product in a production environment, followed by the testing team validating that the launch was successful. Testing teams perform sanity testing on the purchase flows as well as test the core product capability to ensure it is working in production.

Once confirmed the product is successfully launched, you kick off the marketing activities. This typically includes the following:

- o Putting up the product pages: Product pages describe the product functionality, how to set it up and use the product.
- o Putting up the FAQs and support pages
- o Retail teams putting up displays (or other store accessories)
- o Kick off the Marketing plan
  - ▪ Tactics
  - ▪ Sales Enablement
- o Product Demos, Presentations: For B2B products, the product manager needs to have the sales tools ready to enable the sales team to sell the product. This includes the product description document, product demonstrations and sales presentations.
- o Customer Meetings (B2B): Communicate to the sales team to ensure they set up the customer meetings to sell the product leveraging the tools provided above.

Launch Day War Room

You need to ensure you have all the teams available to support the product. As the testing completes and issues are identified, they need to be assessed in severity and if required resolved or logged for future resolution.

As customers purchase the product from the digital store or physical stores and customers start using the product, any issues identified also need to be assessed for severity and resolved or logged for future resolution.

To be able to do that you will need key team members representatives from all the teams involved in building the product and supporting the product to be available on the day of launch and this is the war room (or virtual war room).

As part of the launch go/no-go, you should have the primes needed for war room identified and ensure availability and support for the launch day.

As part of the launch planning, product managers should ensure they have worked with the operational team to ensure post launch support.

If it is a new product, they need to ensure call centers or support centers are able to log tickets associated with those products, the ticket will get routed to the right operational team for resolution.

Dashboards

Depending on the product you will need a number of dashboards, to know how well your product is doing in the market.

Sales dashboard showing how well your sales funnel is working. This could be from SAP (or similar platform for B2B customers) or from your digital page showing number of clicks on product page, add to basket and finally purchase. Depending on your product it might be different, key is to know how well the product is selling.

Operational dashboard reflects how well the product is performing in its usage. Here you measure the number of times it is used, what percentage of usage resulted in success vs. failure, what was the error reported. You should have your technical team looking at the more detailed performance KPIs including latency, uptime etc. as needed for your product success.

Support dashboard should reflect the number of support requests from each channel, what kind of questions are being asked and are the teams able to resolve those issues or does it require system fix.

Marketing dashboards should reflect how successful the marketing efforts are including product sentiment, click through rates etc. per marketing channel.

Having a baseline for each of these products helps identify issues, when you see the graph moving substantially away from the baseline. This would reflect an issue with the product or in the support process or the marketing activities and the product manager should be able to dig deeper to figure out what went wrong and resolve the issue.

This also helps you in building your next business case, it provides a good baseline of usage and that can be leverage for the business. Also as issues are identified, product managers can assess the cost vs. benefit easily to see if it is worth fixing the issue, alternatively combine a number of issues and build the business case for dot release.

Kpis And Success Metrics

As part of your kick off deck and original business case, product managers sign up for specific KPIs and success metrics. Usually are related to

- Product Delivery
- Product Performance
- Sales

The dashboards you build in the previous section, would help you measure how you are progressing towards your KPIs and success metrics.

Ideally this gives a product manager an opportunity to improve performance of the product (and personal performance) by identifying issues earlier in the year and having time to implement changes to improve the metrics.

CHAPTER 7:
TURN DOWN

At some point a product manager has to make a decision on should investment continue in the current product or do they need to stop investment. This is largely driven by the dashboards/KPIs above, combined with the organization strategy, market trends etc.

Product Managers have multiple options at this stage of the product, they are

- Extend or Pivot the product Line
- Sell the product line to another company
- Stop and Kill the product

Which of the above options is selected depends on the company strategy to a large extent.

Extend The Product Line

Extending the product line is expanding it to another vertical, re-purposing the product for another solution or pivoting from the product line to a similar product (leveraging the same base code, knowledge, resources etc.)

To be able to successfully extend the product line, the product manager also needs to perform the following:

- Communicate to customers about the upcoming plans, discuss the upgrade options, pricing and support options.
- End of Life communications include communicating the End of Life date (no further new development), end of sale date (sales team will no longer carry this product beyond that date), end of support date (beyond which date no support will be offered).

For a successful turn down, have a strong focus on your communication plan. Communicate often, be clear and respond to any clarification questions.

Clear communications will help you retain your customers and open new opportunities for B2B sales.

Sell The Product Line

Typically along with the product line, you are also selling the customer base. The company acquiring your product might be doing it to consolidate their market share, or buying the relationships with the clients.

To be able to structure this right, the Product Manager has to have an estimate of potential future sales and the net present value of those sales, value of the relationship with the customers as well as the base cost of building the product.

The value you associate with the actual sale would be based on the above three and then get negotiated. Depending on if the team that developed and supports the product is moving on not, will also need to be factored into the pricing structure.

Stop And Kill The Product Line

If the cost of support is high and future potential sales are low, and you cannot find any interested buyers of the product, the right decision might be to kill the product line.

The product manager might assess the strategic value of the product being low compared to other products and choose to kill a product. If this product will still getting sales, be prepared for resistance from the sales team as they would like to continue selling a product if they can, you need to look beyond quarterly sales at the strategic value.

CHAPTER 8: CHALLENGES OF PRODUCT MANAGEMENT

Product managers need to be aware of a number of blind spots and ensure they cover these blind spots to make their products (and careers successful).

- Core team representation
- Lack of metrics
- Trade-offs
- Insufficient allocation of time to turn-downs
- Project Management

Core team representation

The product manager needs to ensure representation at the core team has all the right teams involved.

More generally put, for your organization what are the all teams that need to be resented. For a small startup, this will be straight forward, for a large enterprise this could be a large number of teams.

Ensure all the teams have a say and awareness of the planned product during kick off is important. Having the key subset who will work with you on a daily/weekly and will play a critical role in ensuring the product is launched successfully are identified and committed is critical.

Ensure you have a regular (daily standup or weekly core call) touch point with the core team. This keeps the team aligned on the progress, roadblocks, assumptions and compromises made in the product development journey.

Lack of Metrics

A successful product manager should be tracking a lot of KPIs representing different lenses of the product. These typically include

- Revenue
  - Sales Funnel (prospects, leads etc.)
- Usage
  - How often is the product being used (downloads, logins, transactions, purchases, error rates etc.)
  - How successful was the usage (transactions successful, failure rates, error rates with reason codes etc.)
- Customer Experience
  - How many return customers do you have?
  - What is the Net Promoter Score (NPS)? Rating on the app score?
  - Social media sentiment analysis
  - How many calls are you getting for support, and the reason for the call?
- Performance
  - Technical performance of the application like uptime, latency, memory utilization, cpu utilization, number of transactions

As product manager, you should be looking at the baselines of these graphs in a dashboard and digging into significant changes.

Trade Offs

As product manager over the course of development, launch you will need to make many decisions. Most decisions will require you to make a compromise on quality, time, scope or budget.

Leverage your core team to make the best decision, the collective decision likely will be better than an individual decision. Also letting your core team know the constraints might bring out better solutions.

Discuss all options with the core team before making a decision. Also consider the "in the news" article, what if this compromise results in the product making headlines - are you doing the right thing? Especially when making decisions around security, legal, regulatory and privacy decisions.

Take the key decisions to the governance body, use the senior management as the litmus test, would they approve the decision?

Insufficient time allocation to turn downs

Product turndowns should be a focus and not an afterthought. When done right you get to move the customers to a strategically important product or new product, retain the customers, keep competition out and reduce operating expenses.

The turn down should be based on solid metrics (and not an emotional choice).
- What is the revenue forecast?
- What is the cost of selling and maintaining the product? What is the profit margin?
- How many customers are actively using the product?
- How long are the support contracts?

Many product managers only find the new product development exciting. Product Management includes managing the product in market and planning for the future which might include a turn down or expanding the product line.

Project Management

Many times product managers underestimate the value of project managers. Project Managers specialize in managing projects and tracking details like monthly cost variance, tracking actions to completions, ensuring core meeting actions are closed, sending minutes from governance meetings, escalating as required etc.

For a small project or in startups, I have seen the same person play the role of a project and product manager, while it can work it does not scale. For a successful organization, you need to have specialists for both the roles - Project and Product manager.

CHAPTER 9:
NEXT STEPS

This book has walked through the detailed process of kicking off a project to start building the product idea as an MVP and then iterating on building process by having a roadmap of prioritized featured.

It is now your turn to get started on executing one of the product ideas you may have, convert the idea into a MVP, validate it with customer and develop the product roadmap.

Build your product iteratively, get feedback and prioritize your features based on that feedback.

ABOUT THE AUTHOR

Vinay Kumar

Vinay Kumar is a seasoned product execu-
tive with over 23 years of experience in
product management both in startups as
well as large organizations. Mr. Kumar has
extensive experience building product
management teams, establishing and opti-
mizing product management processes and
enabling organizations to become truly
product based companies.

Mr. Kumar is currently working on writing several books in the
product management domain, along with mentoring a number of
product management executives. You can read more of his views
at https://rdgrants.com/

When not busy innovating on products, Mr. Kumar spends his
time with his wife and three kids in Toronto, Ontario.

BOOKS BY THIS AUTHOR

Product Roadmap: Creation And Alignment

A product roadmap is the final artifact that is presented widely in the organization. Building a roadmap is a journey not a one time event. The journey starts surprisingly not with the intent of building a roadmap rather with building a product strategy. This book walks you through all the elements required to build your roadmap as well as different types of roadmaps like visionary roadmap, detailed roadmap, C-level view of the roadmap etc. The book walks you through managing these different roadmaps, and how to align your team and get funding and resources allocated to execute and build the roadmap features.

Product Strategy: Step-By-Step Guide To Building Your Awesome Product Strategy

Product Managers struggle with building a strong, viable and executable product strategy. This book provides a detailed step-by-step guide to building product strategy including providing the tools, but more importantly how to work through your organization to get the required support and buy-in to get the organization aligned to your product strategy and execute on it.

The book covers the pre-work that is required to build the strategy, the first step of which is to ensure you can make time in your busy calendar to build this strategy. Once you have completed the pre-work you will be ready to launch into the actual strategy building phase including Marketing trends, competitive analysis, business case etc. Building strategy takes time, you can rush through these phases and build the first version, as you keep focusing over time on these elements your strategy will get more refined and have stronger support within the organization.

Finally the book walks you through the execution phase, how do you get the resource, funding commitment from the leadership to execute the strategy.